THE OFFICIAL LOAN OFFICER STRATEGY GUIDE

Nick Carpenter

*Ready.
Fire.
Aim.*

Nick

"To create a new standard, you have to be up for that challenge and really enjoy it."

- **Shigeru Miyamoto**, Inventor of Donkey Kong and Mario

Thank you Stewart Hunter for teaching me the importance of relationships, Jim McMahan for inspiring me to create The Legion of Loan Officers, Bryan for always supporting me and Jessika for lifting me up to become the best version of myself.

Nick Carpenter

TABLE OF CONTENTS

1. The First Videos You Need To Shoot — Pg 11
2. Three Ways To Prospect Agents — Pg 20
3. Movie Night With Friends — Pg 25
4. Schedule Go Deep Days — Pg 30
5. One New Client Per Closing — Pg 34
6. Ideas for Google Alerts — Pg 39
7. Video Marketing Equipment — Pg 42
8. The Impressive Birthday Video — Pg 46
9. Shine a Spotlight on Partners — Pg 48
10. Common Questions Library — Pg 52
11. Saturday Morning Pump Up — Pg 55
12. Guess The Price Contest — Pg 59
13. New Listing Follow Up — Pg 62
14. Big Blue Database Ads — Pg 65
15. Capture Ghost Clients — Pg 68
16. Classes Realtors Want — Pg 72
17. Monthly Market Update Video — Pg 78
18. Got $5 On It? — Pg 81
19. Popping Bottles at Closing — Pg 83

20. Lotto Ticket Icebreaker — Pg 85
21. Credit Repair Partner — Pg 88
22. Become a Local Ambassador — Pg 91
23. The Networking Stack — Pg 95
24. El Grupo Gratis — Pg 98
25. Exposure Offer — Pg 103
26. Leads.Leads.Leads. — Pg 107
27. Marketing Checklist — Pg 111
28. Open House Survival Kit — Pg 114
29. Setup For Site Visits — Pg 116
30. Treasure Chest of Ideas — Pg 120
31. Surround Yourself With Winners — Pg 123

STRATEGY #1
RECORDED LOAN PROCESS VIDEOS

There are two series of videos that you should shoot right now as a loan officer. Many parts of the mortgage process when we're dealing with clients or we're helping referral partners, they're repeatable. You find yourself having the same conversations over and over.

One way that you can stop doing that is by creating these two video series.

The first video series is going to be for the public and for your referral partners to use. It's a loan process video series.

What we want to do is break down the mortgage process and the home buying process into about 6-8 steps.

For each step, we want to shoot a video that's 1-3 minutes long explaining exactly what occurs during that part of the process.

You can do these videos yourself as a loan officer. You could also partner with a Realtor and shoot these videos or you could go out and get professionals from each part of the actual process and have them shoot the videos with you.

Once you have these videos done, they can benefit your business for years to come.

You can use them as YouTube videos, Facebook videos, as ads, as information for your database, etc.

They have many uses and you only have to make them one time, which is the best part.

Your first series of videos is going to be public.

Here's an example of what that could look like:

Video 1 – Pre-Approval

Talk about what it actually takes to get pre-approved for a home loan.

You can share the difference between pre-qualification and pre-approval so that the public understands that part and just why it's important to start with a pre-approval versus going out and looking at houses or some of the other steps that people may think you should come first.

You can explain why the preapproval is important as the first step. This of course is going to be the video that you as a loan officer, no matter whether you do it all yourself or you have other people involved, of course, you're going to be on this video as the mortgage professional.

Video 2 – Choose a Realtor

The next video might be about how to choose the Realtor you're going to work with. You can have a Realtor come on or you could chat about what's involved with that, right?

Topics can include –

- How to choose an agent
- Difference between a part time and a full time agent
- Difference between a Realtor and a real estate agent
- Difference between somebody that's a neighborhood expert and has a track record versus somebody that's just willing to come into that area and show you houses
- How to work with a new builder

These are all pieces that could go on video two.

Video 3 – Finding the Right Home

On video number three could be about actually finding the right home.

- Share what's involved with that
- How you go out looking at houses
- How all of the shopping process works
- Needs versus Wants
- How to choose a neighborhood
- Homes vs Townhomes vs Condos

A Realtor would be a great person to talk about this process because they're going to understand it better than just about anybody else.

Video 4 – Executed Contract

Video four could be about actually getting the house under contract.

So your content here is –

- Making the offer

- What's involved in the offer
- Different money pieces you have to come up with
- Earnest money
- Option money
- The inspection period
- When a contract is executed
- What options the seller has

We know the seller has three options.

They can accept the contract, they can reject the contract, or they can make a counteroffer, right?

I guess they have a fourth option because they could technically do nothing. They could just choose to not respond at all to your offer.

That would be the content for video 4 about how to actually get the house under contract.

Video 5 – Home Inspection

Video number five can be about the home inspection and your information can include -

- How an inspection works
- What a home inspection costs
- What they look for
- What they don't look for
- How the report works
- How long it takes
- What you should do as a buyer
- If you should be there or not

Video five is a place where you can answer frequently asked questions about a home inspection.

Video 6 – Home Appraisal

And then video number six is about the appraisal.

- What is an appraisal
- What does an appraiser do
- How do they decide the home's value
- How long does it take to get an appraisal back
- How much does it cost
- Who pays for it

These are all questions that you can answer on video six.

Video 7 – Underwriting / Full Approval

Video seven could be about the underwriting process.

- What does it take to get full approval on a loan
- What are conditions
- How do we clear conditions
- What does full approval mean
- Can you be rejected after being pre-approved
- Credit do's and don'ts

That's what video 7 should cover.

Video 8 – Closing & Getting Keys

And then you could go into talking about closing. So you could have a talk about what happens at closing.

- When do you actually become the homeowner

- When does the money get transferred
- How does the money transfer work from the mortgage company
- When does the buyer get the house keys

Those are questions that you could answer on video 8.

Creating a series like this is really powerful because you can have it live on your YouTube channel.

If you wanted to, you could even create a domain and have a domain pointing to that playlist, like ArlingtonHomebuyerQuestions.com or HowToBuyaHomeinTexas.com or you can get creative with the domain you use. Obviously shorter the better, but like 76015faq.com or something like that would be cool.

Whenever you get a lead, these videos can be part of your automation or part of your drip campaigns. Realtors can also have it as a resource for people coming through open houses.

I would get postcards made with a domain and promote the videos via a postcard that I give to Realtors they can use and pass out at open houses.

Now everybody coming through open houses all get a chance to visit my series on YouTube and we want that.

There's a lot of opportunity around that, whether you have offers in the video description or ask them to contact you. Plus you can do retargeting on YouTube also.

The second series you should create is a series for people actually going through the loan process.

There are a lot of touch points during the mortgage process that you repeat yourself over and over with clients.

Every loan is different but they all have the same steps.

Some of those steps are:

- Receiving a loan application
- Getting them pre-approved
- Buyers get the house under contract
- Getting conditions back from underwriter
- Full approval / Clear to close
- Docs to the title company
- Fully funded / Keys transferred

Those would be seven steps, as examples, that you can have in a video series.

Now with this series, you're not going to make it public. It's going to be on your YouTube channel as Unlisted videos.

The only way people are going to be able to get to these videos is through the links you promote.

Say for example, when you get an application in, you have a typical response back to that customer.

'Hey, thank you so much. We received your application. Here's what you should expect...'

Record that on a quick video.

Make the video as short as you can 45 seconds, 60 seconds. If it has to be longer, you know, absolutely has to be, make it longer, but 60 seconds should be plenty of time to say the things you need to say.

As clients hit different milestones in the mortgage process, when you email them or you text them, or as you have your automations built out to do this, when people move through your pipeline process, you can have cool videos that go out.

So you can say, "Hey, I just got your application. Here's what you can expect next.", and have them click the link to open a YouTube video and now they can watch a video to see you talk.

These clients will get 100% of your communication with hand motions, facial expressions and everything that goes into sharing a message.

So that's a way that you can stop repeating yourself in phone calls or with long emails and it's just a way that you can create a better connection with your clients as they're going through the process because they're constantly getting face to face communication with you.

Even though you're not seeing their face, they're seeing your face. Usually that's enough to create a connection on a human level so they don't go out and rate shop you because now they feel way more connected to you.

Those are two types of video series that you should consider to create for your mortgage business - one that's designed for the public and for your Realtor referral partners to use as bait at open houses or for their leads. And, the second series is for people actually going through your loan process.

So even though you're not meeting with them face to face, they can still see your face every time you're delivering news about their loan without re-creating that content over and over.

STRATEGY #2
3 WAYS TO PROSPECT AGENTS

One of the great things about marketing today is every single person in America that you're going to want to connect with, especially when it comes to real estate agents, they all are on Facebook.

We're going to talk about three different ways that you can prospect Realtors on Facebook using Facebook ads to put yourself in front of them for as little as $1 per day.

Did you know that you can get started using Facebook ads for as little as $1 per day?

Obviously many people are spending way more than that.

Today, my average is between $500 and $800 per day on Facebook ads (visit OneAgentAway.com to learn my ads) and it's an amazing platform with huge potential ROIs if you know what you're doing and your use ads the right way.

So what we're going to do is share three quick ways that you can use Facebook ads to target agents, put your message in front of them and eventually convert them into referral partners.

Idea #1 – Upload a list of Realtors as a custom audience

First, you can upload a list of Realtors that you have already.

If you have a database, there are probably Realtors in it.

In fact, you might even have a separate database of just agents and you can export that list from your CRM and you can import the list into Facebook as a custom audience and then you can run ads to that audience.

This is a concept only a few people are taking full advantage of because you can actually take a list of specific people that you want to target.

In this case, we're talking about doing this with real estate agents and how you can run an ad and only show the ad to people that are on that list.

What you need to do is go into your CRM and you're going to export the list of Realtors and it has to be one of two file types, either a .CSV or a .TXT.

Once you upload the data, Facebook is going to go out and search for those names and emails and cell phone numbers, and try to connect the information on your list with profiles that exist on Facebook. And then it will tell you, you've uploaded 300 leads and it will create an audience off of everybody that it can find from that list.

It usually takes anywhere from 30 minutes to one hour for the list to be fully populated so that you can go run ads to those folks.

This is a cool way you can keep yourself top of mind with Realtors that already know you on some level and you can continue to make yourself more and more known to agents that already know you.

I'm assuming because you have them on a list they already know you from real life or email blasts you're sending. Bringing these people into Facebook as an audience and running videos to them will create a whole new dynamic level to your campaign.

Idea #2 - Drop pins or do geo-targeting on Facebook

Say for example, there are 5 large real estate companies in your local market, you could actually target their office addresses on Facebook or you can drop a pin on top of the building and then you can exclude some other areas so that you only target just their building.

This is a way you can be able to geo-target Realtors or people inside of an office that you know belongs to a real estate company.

Imagine doing this with a ReMax office, for example and you go and you say, "Hey, what's up ReMax Mid Cities? If you've been trying to figure out Facebook ads, I have a class that we're hosting next week and I want to invite you to that and just click the link below and you can get all the information for you. Hope to see you there guys."

That's very powerful video when you can get that specific and targeted in your message, knowing that only people in that building and who belong to that company are going to see your ad.

Idea #3 - Target Realtors on Facebook through the targeting itself

There are two ways you can target real estate agents on Facebook inside the Ads Manager. The first way is by job title. You'll find Realtor, real estate agent, real estate broker and other titles like that you can target inside of Facebook.

You can also target based on their employer. If they work at one of the bigger companies like Keller Williams, Coldwell

Banker, Century 21, EXP or any of the other big national companies, and even sometimes the local companies, they will show up as employers inside the Facebook ads manager and you can target those specific agents.

So, that's three different ways that you can target Realtors on Facebook for as little as $1 per day.

This keeps you relevant in front of those agents so that as you're out at networking events or if you're doing direct response ads, you can be getting more appointments with agents.

It's also a way to demonstrate that you have knowledge about Facebook ads Realtors might not have by simply putting yourself in front of them on Facebook and just doing it as an actual demonstration of your skills.

You'll get some DMs sliding in too from the shy agents who don't want to comment publicly.

STRATEGY #3
HOST A MOVIE NIGHT

Hosting a movie night with a Realtor is an amazing way to get in front of their entire database and give them the opportunity to re-connect face to face with clients they've already done business with. It's very affordable at the same time.

This idea is one I got from Brad Chambliss in Kentucky. He told it's almost always profitable whenever he runs this strategy with his Realtor partners before the event occurs because of the referrals that come in just through the invitation process.

If you read the book *7 Levels of Communication* by Michael J. Maher, he talks about the communication pyramid or whatever he calls it; maybe it's the communication triangle. Anyhow, there are two zones for this triangle. One is the communications zone and one is the influential zone.

Hosting a movie night is a way to help you and the Realtors go from being in the communication zone with their database to make an influential zone.

You're getting an opportunity to send out handwritten note cards. You're going to get an opportunity to make a personal phone calls and you're going to be hosting an event so that you can actually get face to face, which is the ultimate way to be influential - to host events.

So there are a few pieces that you need to understand in order to be able to pull off a movie night.

Step 1 – Get a Date and Location

The first question is where are you going to do it and how does it actually the logistics work.

Go to your local movie theater and ask them what their slowest day of the week is and particularly what is their slowest evening of the week. Usually that's going to be a Monday, Tuesday or Wednesday. Tell them you'd like to rent a theater and have all of your clients come in and be able to watch a movie. You also want them all to get a small popcorn and coke.

Get a package price with the movie theater in order to be able to do that for probably $5 - $10 per person. So that way that's all inclusive of the movie ticket, the small drink and the small popcorn for each person coming to the event.

You need to arrange that first and once you get the logistics taken care of where you know the date, the time, the movie, and that everybody's going to get the small popcorn and small drink, and then you can go and have an invitation created.

I like to use the Willy Wonka golden ticket as an example of the invitation and have invites created based off of that. Then what we're going to do is mail one per household. You don't have to mail one per person, if it's a family of four, it's just one per household.

There's a lot of companies out there you can have create the invitation for you. Look online or ask your local printer if that's something that they can help you with or of course, you could hire a college student or a high school student or somebody to put all the invitations together, handwrite the address on the outside and get them in the mail.

Step 2 – Arrange a Photographer and Backdrop

Now what you want to do is set up for photos at the event and you'll need two pieces.

You need a photographer.

Have the Realtor look through their own database and find a photographer that would be willing to come out and shoot a couple of photos per family. Obviously if the photographer will do it for free, then that's awesome. Tell them that they can watermark the pictures and it'll benefit them.

If you have to pay them, then obviously there should be no watermark if you're paying the photographer to be there.

Once you secure a photographer, you want to get an artist to create a step and repeat banner like they use at red carper premier events. These can be printed and shipped to you from several eBay sellers. It will tell you all the sizes, dimensions and everything you need to know for the artists and it will come with a banner stand as well.

As the families come to the movie theater, you can have the step and repeat banner set up in the lobby or right outside of your actual movie room and the photographer can take pictures of each family. That's a really cool souvenir.

What you do with those pictures is once the photographer's done? Have the Realtor create a photo album with all the pictures on their business page or personal profile.

Then they can send out an email to the database with a link to the photo album and ask people to comment, like, and share the photos from the event and it's going to basically create a viral effect of sharing that photo album. The photographer will get a lot of exposure, like we talked about, we want to make sure that they get tons of value.

Overall, it's a pretty simple event to pull off. All you have to do is plan the logistics, get an invitation created and mailed out to their database and then find a photographer for the step and repeat banner and get the step and repeat banner creative.

And like Brad says, "You will always get referrals just from the invitations."

Sometimes people that can't come, they will want to call you and let you know that or you just become top of mind again with the database so that you can be able to receive those referrals. You might say that we're even initiating the law of reciprocity by bringing their entire family out for a movie night with free drinks and free popcorn. And now they're like, what can I give them back? The natural answer is a referral for somebody else that wants to buy or sell a house or somebody else that needs a mortgage or needs to refinance a mortgage.

Think about doing a movie night with a Realtor. It's simple and has amazing results every time I've seen it happen and you can be the next success story for the Realtor-Loan Officer movie night.

STRATEGY #4
GO DEEP DAYS

A lot of marketing today is focused on broad marketing.

We talk a lot about targeting large groups of people with Facebook ads or sending out an email to the entire database or writing a Facebook post to thousands of friends at the same time or even hosting a class with 15 or 20 Realtors in the room at the same time.

That type of connection where it's a "one to many" connection is going to create one type of relationship or one layer to a relationship, but in order to create a really deep meaningful relationship, there has to be one on one moments of connection.

This is also true for business relationships.

The idea of Go Deep Days is to create that one on one connection opportunity with your referral partners.

A Go Deep Day is going to cost some money. Usually they will cost anywhere from $500 to $2,000 depending on what you're doing.

You might stay local and do a one day thing or it could become a whole weekend of fun flying to somewhere else.

When I say a one on one connection, it doesn't necessarily mean you have to be only one on one with a Realtor. That is the best case scenario but it could also be one Realtor and their family along with your family going out camping for a weekend or something along those lines, right?

It's about creating an opportunity to build relationships at a deeper level. People will talk and say things one on one that they would never say in front of a group.

You can learn about people's problems, fears, challenges, successes, what they're proud of, all these kinds of things that they may not want to ever reveal in front of a group.

So a group is amazing to build a surface level and starting to build on a meaningful relationship but these one on one moments of connection is what's really going to build that a for you and for your partners.

Sally and the Oreos

There's a great example from a loan officer named Sally in Tennessee and there was a female Realtor Sally wanted to get the business from named Nik.

And Nik, she was a well known agent in town and Sally knew she was going to have to do something really special to get her attention and to be able to have the opportunity to earn that business.

So Sally used a really cool way to guarantee you have someone's attention.

First, she went on Nik's Facebook profile and through doing some digging and researching, she found out Nik had a secret passion for Oreos. Like late at night, she would go sneak a couple of Oreos.

Sally searched around and found an Oreo bowl that is divided where you can put your cookies in one half and your milk in the other half and it's a special dish just for people who love Oreos.

She bought the bowl and some Oreos and she had it wrapped up really nice and she sent it to Nik as just an attention getter and it worked really well.

They started working together some, but Sally was not Nik's only lender. She wasn't the only person that was getting those referrals and she wanted to figure out how to make that happen.

Boot'n & Shoot'n

From knowing Nik for a few months and having that relationship with her, Sally knew that Nik was really big into supporting law enforcement and the military. She liked shooting guns and country music and these kinds of things.

There's a big charity event that occurs in Dallas every year called Boot'n & Shoot'n, so Sally invited Nik to come down and attend that event, so they did.

They came down together and Sally took care of the flight, the hotel, the event tickets, everything like that and made it really a first class special opportunity for Nik.

Sally could have easily invited multiple referral partners to come, but it wasn't about multiple people. It was about that one relationship and what could happen through grow growing that one relationship in a significant way.

Sally and Nik came down to Texas for the event and it's a big country music event with skeet shooting and an auction. There are tons of military veterans and even special guests that are amputees and Special Forces and just a lot of bad ass guys.

By coming to that event, Sally and Nik had an opportunity to connect one on one. They had an opportunity to go deeper in their relationship than they ever had an opportunity to do back home.

They had lots of time to talk on the plane, in the car, at the event itself, in the car again, on the plane again.

There's a lot of opportunity to talk and get to know each other and not even necessarily just talk about business but just what are your values, your passions, what are your commitments? Where's your integrity? What are your priorities? These kinds of things that you want to know about people that you're going into business with.

That simple gesture of an Oreo bowl, that seems so silly, and by inviting Nik to a charity event about the things that she cared about the most, Sally was able to earn her business and become Nik's referral partner of choice.

Consider how you can use deep dive days in your business so that you can build deeper, more meaningful one on one relationship with the Realtors that matter the most to you.

STRATEGY #5
GET 1 NEW CLIENT PER CLOSING

Today in America and probably in the whole world, we trust other people's reviews and opinions more than we trust advertising.

I personally blame Amazon for this, and we even call it the Amazon effect inside of the Legion of Loan Officers (LegionofLoanOfficers.com) because of how powerful they've been able to create the five star review.

When you go to Amazon and you look at any items that's for sale, it's going to show you how many people reviewed it, what the review is, what they said about the item, how many people bought that or what they bought instead, what they also bought with it, right?

There are so many layers to the social proof that's created on Amazon so you have to ask yourself, how many layers of social proof are you creating in your business?

One way you can add them is by getting customer reviews from every single closing you have.

There are two different types of reviews you can get online. The first is a written review; the second is a video testimonial.

Video is always harder to get than written reviews.

Getting Video Reviews

So first I'm going to share how you can get a video testimonial from every time that you have a closing. This has a two step process and it has to start the night before closing.

What you want to do is call your client and ask them, "hey client, I'm so excited to go to closing with you tomorrow. It's going to be awesome. I can't wait. Let me ask you this, when we first started working together, what were you the most nervous about? What was the most concerning to you?"

They're going to tell you what that was. Maybe that they couldn't qualify and they didn't have enough down payment. They wouldn't be able to get in the neighborhood they want to live in, etc.

Then you can ask them this, "how did I help you overcome that fear or that challenge?"

And, they'll answer and thank them for that information.

Next, you'll ask, "I'm wondering if tomorrow, since I'm going to be there at closing, and you know in today's world having customer reviews is such an important thing, that I'm wondering if I set my camera up on a little tripod, would you be willing to tell that story tomorrow or just talk about the process of buying this house and getting the home loan with me? Would you be willing to share that on video tomorrow? Because the reason I ask you is I know there's so many people that if they hear your story, they'll be able to connect to it. Would you be willing to do that for me?"

Almost 100% of the time you're going to get a yes.

Then at closing, you just pull out your little tripod and put your phone in there.

Every person in America knows how to start and stop a camera on a cell phone at this point. So leave the room and let them give you a testimonial that's super genuine.

When you come back, now you've got a great video testimonial to use in your marketing. You can put that on YouTube, you can put it on your website, and you can use it on Facebook ads. There are tons of opportunities with that video.

Getting Written Reviews

A few days after closing we can ask for a written review online.

We'll send an email and say something like –

Hey, thank you so much again for trusting me for your mortgage advice.

It was an honor to serve you.

You know that reviews are super important today. People are constantly out there Googling and checking to see how many five star reviews we have online and I'm wondering if you could just help us add to that.

I've shared 3 links below. Pick whichever one or multiples that you feel comfortable leaving reviews on.

It would mean so much to me.

Link 1

Link 2

Link 3

Thank you again,

Signature

This simple email will get you tons of reviews.

You could even include some examples so you can show them what a great written review looks like online. Sometimes people need a little inspiration, especially if it's not something they're used to doing.

You can slowly, but with lasting results, start taking over online by having reviews on Google, Yelp, Facebook, Zillow, and Realtor.com. The social proof stacks up and people can't help but to find you organically or be reinforced to hire you when they're out there searching for you because their friends said you were amazing.

Video testimonials are a great way to have that same proof on Facebook and Instagram and YouTube to reinforce how great you are.

That's one way you can get a client from every single closing you have is by getting a video testimonial the day of closing and asking them to leave a couple of reviews online for you about a week after closing. Give them a little bit of time to get settled in the house before you ask for online reviews.

STRATEGY #6
GOOGLE ALERTS

Anybody can write anything they want on the internet and unless you have an entire army of people out there and trying to search for what people are saying about you, it's practically impossible to actually stay on top of it.

One tool that exists, that does make this a little bit easier is Google Alerts.

Alerts is a free tool that is provided by Google you can set up to receive alerts either in real time or once a day with any new information online that has the keywords or the phrases that you tell them you want to be notified about.

Some of the ways that you can use Google Alerts are:

1. For your own business

You can set up Google alerts for your name, your company name, your NMLS number, your email address, your cell phone number, and your office phone number.

These are all potential Google Alerts you could set up and get a once a day or real time notifications. That way if anybody is using your information on a website online or mentioning you in a YouTube video description or even some social posts that could mention you, Google Alerts will find them and they will actually alert you and let you know through an email with a link to whatever it is that they found online.

It's a great way you can protect yourself. It's a great way you can protect your business. It's also a way you can monitor for SEO. For example, if you are actively creating content online and you want to find out when that content ranks on Google, you could create a Google Alert for the title or keywords you want to rank for.

2. For your referral partners' businesses

The other way you can use Google Alerts is to set up alerts for your referral partners so you can look for their name, their real estate team name, their cell phone number or their office phone number would be some examples.

Google will send you a once per day email you can breeze through or have an assistant do it.

How cool would it be if somebody writes an article about the top 10 Realtors in the city and you find it before the Realtor even knows about it and you're able to send it to them and say, "congratulations for being featured in this article!" and they're like, wow, I had no idea that even happened.

Those are some of the uses for Google Alerts.

It's a really great free tool that will help you to stay on top of anything people are saying about you, good or bad online or on social media or in videos.

And, you can also do the same thing for your referral partners, which is a really cool value add.

STRATEGY #7
VIDEO MARKETING EQUIPMENT

In America, there's a whole concept of keeping up with the Jones' and you see that happen as well with video marketing equipment.

People think they need the latest camera, a mirrorless camera, or the latest GoPro, or the latest iPhone in order to be able to shoot quality videos.

The reality is that whatever cell phone you carry in your pocket today has all the capabilities and technology that you need to make high quality videos that other people will want to watch and listen.

Of course, there's always going to be ways to improve. You can always get new equipment. You can always upgrade and improve your tripod or your camera or your microphone or your video editing software. There will always be room for improvement, but most people are waiting on the sidelines until they have the perfect video equipment, which probably doesn't even exist in order to start making videos.

What you need to know is that's just an excuse.

It's just a delay because if you have any modern iPhone or Android phone, the camera and the microphone inside of that cell phone are plenty good in order to shoot videos to market your mortgage business.

So, don't let the idea of needing the best video equipment hold you back from starting to shoot videos.

Get started with your cell phone and then as you're making progress and you're shooting content on a regular basis, perhaps you could even reward yourself after you make a certain number of videos and then go buy some better equipment.

Once you're already taking action and you're creating momentum and you're making progress, then you can look at upgrading your camera equipment.

For the equipment, I recommend using a Manfrotto tripod. They have different versions, but that's just the brand that I prefer. I have a Manfrotto tripod that's designed for DSLR cameras and I have a Manfrotto tripod that's a small one for a cell phone and both of them are really high quality and work really well. They are a little bit more expensive than some of the other ones you might find on Amazon for example, but the quality difference is worth the price difference.

When it comes to cameras, people have all kind of preferences on cameras and what I would suggest is you go to Best Buy or your local camera store and physically hold the cameras and physically touch and manipulate and play with the cameras.

See how it feels in your hands.

See which one is the most comfortable.

See which one has the best hand grip and is easiest to hold.

The 2nd decision to make is getting a camera lens. The lens is going to make the video even better with the blurry background and that kind of thing depending on which one you pick.

I don't recommend buying a camera online because you're not sure how it's going to feel in your hands, if it's going to be comfortable or if the buttons are in weird places.

These are the kinds of things you can only find out by going to the store and physically touching the cameras and finding the one that's going to work best for you.

Once you have a tripod and the camera, you're also going to want to have a microphone.

There are a lot of options for microphones like every other camera accessory.

You can start out using a really simple lavaliere mic. So for example, there's a brand Audio-Technica and they have a lavaliere mic you can get started with for only around $30.

If you want to step up and get a more professional mic, you could get a Rode Mic. I use the Rode Pro+ mic and it has a really long battery life. You can make adjustments depending if it's really loud around you or not and the microphone automatically turns off when you turn your camera off. I really like those features.

The Rode Pro+ microphone is a little bit more expensive than some of the others, but I felt like it was worth it for the long battery life and the automatic shut off. I liked those two features the most.

Again, do not wait to start making videos when you have that equipment.

Start today.

Start now with your cell phone. Use your cell phone.

You can get a small tripod to set your phone on or use it to make selfie videos in your hand.

    But the main thing is to get started now and you can continually improve your equipment a little bit at a time.

STRATEGY #8
FACEBOOK BIRTHDAY VIDEOS

One of the coolest things about Facebook is every single day they remind you of whose birthday it is for your friends, and they're going to make a suggestion to go and write on that person's wall and say happy birthday or leave some sort of a birthday message.

The challenge with is that all their other friends are also doing the same thing. So even if you leave a video or a photo or a gif or a witty comment on their timeline, it gets lost in the shuffle.

It gets lost in the in the mix and the noise, because there's hundreds if not thousands of birthday messages coming through on the person's timeline. Most people can't keep up with it all.

One way you can stand out and be completely different and have a message on people's birthday that's impactful, is to send a video message through Facebook Messenger.

This is a really simple strategy that you can do in only 15 seconds per person that has a birthday.

So, you go into Facebook Messenger on your cell phone and you find the person whose birthday is today.

Once you do that, there's a camera icon and you can click the icon and you can hold the button down and record up to 15 second videos.

What you do is hold the button down and say something like –

"Hey name, happy birthday. I hope today's awesome and people are treating you like a king or queen, and I hope you have a great birthday, happy birthday."

It's a really short, simple, easy message.

Obviously don't say king or queen, pick which one is appropriate there.

This is a video message that's going to have an impact and they're going to watch the video.

Your Facebook friend is going to see you, your face, your smile, and your emotions and it's going to stand out because nobody else is sending video messages on people's birthday.

They're just writing the text on the timeline, which has way less impact, way less emotion, and it's also not memorable at all.

What you are going to do is memorable, is impactful and will create emotions.

So try that as you see Facebook reminding you of your friends' birthdays and send out 15 second happy birthday videos inside Facebook Messenger.

STRATEGY #9
PARTNER SPOTLIGHT

One of the best things you can offer somebody today is exposure. Today, having attention equals currency in the social world that we operate in.

If you can offer somebody exposure to your network on your platforms, it's a big deal and it will be an ego stroke and it will make people feel awesome just simply for you inviting them to have that opportunity.

This Partner Spotlight can be done really simply today using Facebook Live and then taking that Facebook Live, downloading it and uploading it to YouTube as well.

You want to have them in both places so let's talk about how you want to roll this out.

When you do a Facebook Live and you're going to interview a person live, you want to do it from your cell phone with the phone turned horizontally. That way you and your guests are side by side, not with the picture-in-picture where one person's picture is really big and one person is really small in the corner.

If you go live from your cell phone and you'd have it turned horizontally, you guys can be side by side like equals and it makes for a really great video on Facebook.

When you go live on Facebook, the number one objective is to get people to watch the video.

Think about that when you're writing the text that's going to be above the video.

When you're going live, maybe ask a funny question or what would you do in this situation?

You just want to peak somebody's curiosity so that they actually will go in and start watching the live video and interacting during the live session.

During the live video, as many times as you can without being obnoxious, but over and over ask people to pos a comment.

For example, you could say –

- Leave a #live or #replay
- Tell me yes or no to this question
- Have you ever done this before? Yes or no?
- Drop me a comment right now about this...

You can use those comments because knowing that 80% or 90% of your viewers are going to come on a replay, every time those comments are coming in, it pushes the post back up in the newsfeed and as the post comes back in the newsfeed, every time it looks more and more popular.

People that might have ignored it in the beginning when it only had 100 views, as it comes floating back up and flows back up, eventually maybe they watch the video because they're like, okay, I see that 1,000 people have watched this now, or it has 200 comments. Let me jump in here and see what's going on.

And, it's that "Amazon Effect" where eventually that popularity makes them feel like, okay, I got to see what's happening here.

Bring a partner on your Facebook Live and do a Partner Spotlight for them.

Talk about how they got in a real estate business, what their team looks like today, where they live, and why they choose to live in that neighborhood or that city, what are their favorite things about it. These kinds of things, right?

You just want to be able to help connect them to the local community, make them look like an expert and make them look awesome.

Also try to put in some humor. So if you can, you know, maybe you ask them what's the funniest listing appointment they ever had or what's the craziest thing that's ever happened when showing houses.

You want to give some opportunity to let them show their personality and everybody likes to laugh together. You always want to create opportunities to laugh together. And, you can do that with your questions. The questions that you ask will determine what that person is able to say or the direction they go. So, feel free to kind of steer them in ways that they can tell some of those stories, they can share some of those experiences, and they can create an opportunity to laugh.

Once you do the Facebook Live, make sure you hit the share button and not the delete button so it's stays on Facebook and doesn't disappear.

Ideally the Realtor will share your post later and if you have any sort of groups that you use to help each other out and share each other's posts, they can give you some engagement as well.

Once that's over, you can download the video from Facebook and then you could upload it as a video into your YouTube channel.

Now you've got double or even triple coverage because you've got coverage on Facebook, you've got coverage on YouTube, the YouTube video will bleed over into Google so you've got multiple coverage from one video interview.

That's one of the ways you can spotlight a partner today where it's totally free and you're just simply giving them a shout out and some promotion in front of your network and making them look like a super expert.

And, it sort of initiates the law of reciprocity where now they feel like, what can they give you back.

You just gave them so much exposure and so much of a boost and words of encouragement and these things, what can they give you back, and naturally, that's home buyers in this business relationship.

So think about that.

How can you spotlight partner?

What can you do to bring more awareness to them, into your network or give them an opportunity to shine? That's what the Partner Spotlight is all about.

STRATEGY #10
COMMON QUESTIONS DATABASE

Home buyers who are getting a mortgage and just getting started often have lots of the same questions.

Many of them have the same concerns around how the process works, some of the terminology and what they should expect.

One option you have is to create a common mortgage questions database that you can use on Facebook and YouTube. Once you create these videos, now you have holograms of yourself out there selling your services to people that have that exact question you are answering for them.

It's a very powerful strategy that very few loan officers put into place.

But, it's one you should definitely consider doing because it's a one-time effort with long-term payoff and we're always looking for that in marketing.

So what should you create in your common questions database?

Well, if you look back at the last month's worth of emails, conversations, in-person appointments, and Facebook messages, you'll see what people are asking you.

Jot those questions down.

It's going to all be the same 10, 15, 20 questions over and over and over, right?

Here are some examples you could use to get started –

- What is earnest money?
- How much earnest money do I have to put down?
- Where does the closing occur?
- Do buyers & sellers close on a home at the same time?
- What's the difference in different mortgage products.
- What's the difference between a USDA and a FHA?
- What's the difference between FHA & Conventional?
- What is an escrow account and what goes in there?
- Who pays my homeowner's insurance?
- What is PMI?
- When can I stop paying PMI?

These are all some examples of questions that you can answer on video and be able to have a specific answer to a specific question and solve it for anybody who is out there looking on YouTube or Google.

Imagine being able to sit in your neighborhood and have a little booth open for real estate and mortgage questions. Anytime somebody has a question, they can come up to your booth and ask you the question and get an immediate answer.

It's a great idea but probably not the best use of time for you, physically.

Now, imagine having a robot or a hologram monitoring that booth instead of you. That's what you can create on YouTube.

You can create an army of holograms of yourself answering questions 24/7 anytime somebody asks the questions you answer.

It's so powerful because you only have to record the video once and now it's going to answer that question for the next five years or more.

And, when you can help solve a problem for somebody it initiates the law of reciprocity where they feel like, 'what can I do for this person?'

It's also an easy way to transition somebody from answering their questions and helping to solve their problems into, 'hey if you want to know more about working together or how I can help you specifically, here's what's next'.

It's easy to have that as a call to action at the end of your videos and you want to make sure to include it.

Finally, you can also take your YouTube videos and use them for Facebook posts or ads.

Download the video from YouTube and upload it natively to Facebook. Facebook will restrict your reach with a YouTube video and extend your reach with a Facebook video. Those two platforms aren't enemies but they also aren't trying to send them traffic.

The Facebook video posts are good to use in Facebook ad campaigns and for retargeting ads too.

STRATEGY #11
SATURDAY MORNING MESSAGE

The busiest Realtors are working on Saturdays. You already know this. It's a time when families and people who work during the week have the availability to go out and look at houses.

So, it's very common that your real estate partners are probably out showing houses on the weekend while you're at home relaxing with your family or just in general not working.

One of the ways you can remind Realtors you are a team and that you're working and available is to reinforce it on Saturday morning.

Now, there are two ways that you can do this message.

Text Messages

The first way is you can send it as an actual text message.

You can text each Realtor one at a time and with a short message that says –

"Hey, I hope if you're showing any buyers this weekend, you find them exactly what they're looking for. If you get any new buyers you need to get preapproved or you get any new listings that you want to generate leads for, just shoot me a message and I can help you out with that. Hope you have a great weekend."

It's a short reinforcement. It's a positive message letting they know that you're available.

Sometimes they're probably wondering if they can contact you and you want to let them know you are available if they have something that's important and they have a buyer that needs to be pre-approved you will be able to help them out over the weekend.

So that's the first way is to send a text message.

Facebook Messenger

The second way you can do the Saturday Morning Message is using Facebook messenger.

Inside of Facebook Messenger, you would go to the person you want to send the message to and send them the same message you would text –

"Hey John, I hope you have an awesome weekend. If you're showing any buyers, I hope you find them exactly what they're looking for. If you get any new buyers or any new listings that you need to help with getting buyers preapproved or getting leads for your new listing, just let me know and I got you. Have an awesome weekend."

It's an easy way to remind them you're available.

Video Message

Inside the Facebook Messenger, if you want to step it up one notch, do it as a video message.

Instead of sending the message with text, click the camera icon and hold down the circle to record a 15 second video.

Now the other person is going to get all your communication. They're going to get your hand motions, your voice, your eyebrow movements, your smile and all the pieces of communication to create a great connection.

Even if you don't actually talk to the Realtor or they just respond with a thumbs up, they're going to have watched your video and that's what matters.

Consider doing these messages on Saturday mornings as a reminder to the Realtors you already work with.

You can also send these messages to your Realtor hit list if you keep one. These are 10-20 agents you'd love as partners and keep in front of. (Not with those silly Monday calls)

You never know what can happen where one day their Loan Officer pisses them off or they aren't available and you are.

Reminding them you are around can be the shot you need to earn that Realtor's business.

Sending Facebook video messages will keep you top of mind and it's a great point of connection even if it's only occurring one way. 99% of the time Realtors aren't going to send you a video message back so the connection is really only occurring one way.

It's the same kind of connection that fans build with actors or musicians.

It's called a Para-Social Relationship and video on Facebook is the easiest way for you to put this into place for your mortgage business.

STRATEGY #12
GUESS THE PRICE CONTEST

One way real estate agents who are getting listings can generate a ton of interest in the property before it ever goes live in the MLS is using this 'Guess The Price Contest'.

It's a really simple strategy to pull off and what you're going to do is rely on Facebook as a platform. You can also do this on Instagram if the Realtor has a really strong following on Instagram as well.

For most agents, this is going to be best done on Facebook.

It's an easy post to make on Facebook because Realtors are already used to putting videos on Facebook and so this is a simple one to pull off.

What you want to do is right after the listing gets taken, you can either make a video from in front of the house or maybe there's one feature inside of the property that's just really epic and you can show that off and basically you make that as a post on Facebook as a video post.

Above the video, you tell people it's a guess the price contest –

"Post your best guess of what this 4 bedroom home in Arlington with 3,000 square feet and a backyard like a resort will be listed for next week. Guess the price and whoever gets closest in the next 24 hours is going to win a $50 gift card to Bob's Chophouse. If you want a bonus entry to win, share the video and we're going to give away a $50 gift card to somebody that shares the video also."

You could do less on the gift cards if you don't want to do $50, you could do $20 gift cards, $25 gift cards. You might be really surprised at how little money you actually have to offer in order to get people excited about a contest in winning something for free.

This strategy is designed to get interest in the home before it goes live in the MLS and the Realtor has a chance to double end the deal.

You can do this with any property. When the Realtor puts the coming soon sign, they can also do a guess the price post on Facebook with a video either in front of the house or with the best feature behind them.

If there's an awesome pool or rec room or master bath, whatever that is, the best feature is what you want to use on the video. If video is not an option, you can just take a few photos and put four or five photos as a collage on one Facebook post and use those as the bait for people to guess the price.

STRATEGY #13
SHARE LISTINGS ON FACEBOOK

One simple way you can get the attention of a real estate agent on Facebook is to share one of their listings.

Realtors always share their listings on Facebook, especially the agents who don't get very many listings.

If you look at the post a Realtor will make, when they share the property, it's usually going to have some text and a link either to their website or to the MLS where you can go and view the rest of the property. Because of that, they tend to not get very much interaction.

It might have a few likes, maybe some comments, probably not any shares. So, if you share the post when the Realtor has shared a listing, it's noticeable. It stands out. The Realtors will be aware that you've done it because they will get a notification that you shared their listing.

Now when you share the property, if you really want to create interaction, use some sort of fear of missing out (or FOMO) line.

When you make the post on Facebook, tell people they have to check out a certain feature. Like –

"Oh my gosh, you're not going to believe how big this bathtub is!"

"Wait until you check out what's inside the garage!"

"Wait until you see this backyard!"

That kind of sentence on a post is going to make people want to click in and actually go see the property.

If the Realtor is directing the traffic to their own website and they're savvy enough to have installed a Facebook pixel, the good news is you can help them add people to their retargeting.

All the people who click over to see the property are now going to be caught up in that Realtor's retargeting and there's a chance that somebody might go over and see the property and reach out to the agent. Somebody might see your post and want to go view the property. You just never know what can happen from putting information in front of people. Sometimes the right person is going to see it at the right time and it's going to create that connection, otherwise you're just simply giving them some exposure and that has value in itself.

A few days after you share the Realtor's listing, you can send them a Facebook message and say, "Hey, how's it been going with marketing that property on Facebook? I saw your post and shared it. I saw it got a little bit of interaction. Did anyone reach out? Have you been getting any leads for that house on Facebook?"

That's when you can introduce the idea of helping them.

Maybe you can run a Facebook ad and help them generate some leads or you can share some different ideas that you might have on how they could be able to market the property more effectively or use it to generate the most amount of interest and the most amounts of buyers for their database while it's still active.

That's the power of just simply sharing the listing.

Yes, you're just sharing a post.

It's a really easy two step process, but it means a lot and to a Realtor, you're creating exposure for them. You're getting them eyeballs and attention and you're giving them the opportunity to get more business and that's what creates value in the eyes of someone else. It's the opportunity.

It doesn't always have to end in business for there to be a value.

I mean, anytime somebody refers me, it means a lot. It's a big deal to receive a referral and even when that referral doesn't work; it's the fact that somebody created that connection. The value is in the connection.

So, keep that in mind and why you want to consider sharing a listing for a Realtor you've been trying to work with as a way to open the door into a deeper conversation.

STRATEGY #14
FACEBOOK DATABASE ADS

Every loan officer has a database, even though most of us don't market it as often as we probably should.

Actually, ask yourself that right now, when is the last time you emailed your database? When is the last time your database saw your face? When is the last time your database heard your voice?

These are all things that we can solve by running database ads on Facebook.

The amount of information that Facebook has about people and what's available inside the Ads Manager, it can be scary if you are just a consumer.

That's why you want to take full advantage of the information while we can and be able to run ads and use the information existing in there.

One of the things you can do inside the Facebook Ads Manager is creating custom audiences.

The first thing you want to do is login into your CRM and export your database. We really only need their emails and cell phone numbers.

Then, you can upload that list into Facebook and Facebook will create an audience based off of only your uploaded database.

Next, you can run an ad and have it only seen by the people on your list. Sure, people can share the video or ad but you'll only be paying to show it to people who already know you on some level.

This is one of the cheapest, most effective ways to market on Facebook.

Sometimes you'll hear this kind of thing called retargeting, but this is simply a way to stay in front of your database for $1 to $5 per day. You could run these videos all the time.

Staying in front of your database on Facebook is a great supplement to what you're doing in email.

Say for example, you email your database once a week. You could reinforce that message on live video.

So you could get on video and say, "hey, just wanted to let you know I just sent out an email with some information for you and feel free to reach out if you have any questions about that. Hope you're having an awesome day and a great week and month and let me know if there's anything that I can do for you".

These kind of videos where you put in a more human touch and stay in front of folks is a great way to just continually build relationships with your database.

Even if it's only one way and they're only seeing your videos and you're never really seeing videos from them, it's a way that you're going to continue to at least stay top of mind with your database.

Consider using Facebook Ads and uploading your database from inside of your CRM into the Facebook Ads Manager to run videos or events or any other type of Facebook ad and know that they only people who were going to see that ad are people who already know, like, and trust you.

STRATEGY #15
CAPTURE GHOST CLIENTS

We came up with this phrase a few years ago called "Ghost Clients" and the idea is there are people who could become clients and you don't even know they exist yet.

Here's a great example of how this can occur:

Let's say you sell a home with Betty and she is at work and hears her coworker talking about their lease is expiring and they're thinking about getting a house. So Betty introduces your name and gives her coworker your business card.

From that point, Betty's coworker can either decide to do a couple of different things. She could call you directly, which of course is our number one preference. That's what we would like all referrals to do is to reach out to us right away. Or she might want to go do some research before calling you.

Her research probably includes going to Google and see what people are saying about you. She might go to different websites like Zillow, Realtor.com, Yelp, and Google Maps to see what past clients say.

Hopefully the coworker decides to reach out to you based on what they find online.

If not, you'll never know they existed.

Maybe the next day, Betty reaches out to you and says, "hey, I gave your number to this lady at work", and she gives you her coworker's information.

Of course this is the kind of referrals we want the most. We're all excited and call Betty's coworker and she doesn't answer the phone.

What do most people do when a phone number they don't recognize comes in?

They Google it. They go to Google and they type in the phone number and they see what shows up in their results.

One way you can affect those results and you can immediately let people know who you are is by having a YouTube video showing up for your cell phone number.

This is a super easy strategy.

All you need to do is hold your cell phone horizontally and record a 60 second video that says something like this script right here.

"Hey, did you just Google 555-777-8899? Hey, that's me, Nick Carpenter. I'm a loan officer at XYZ Mortgage Company and I probably just reached out to you to talk about a home loan or you might have seen one of our Facebook ads and responding to that or maybe we already know each other and you just didn't recognize my number, so feel free to give me a call back. There's a chance I'm going to be reaching back out to you and you can save my number so that way you'll know who it is calling next time and we can be able to chat. I hope you're having a great day. Talk with you soon."

That's the simple script you're going to record on video.

Then upload the video to YouTube using the app.

Be sure to add a title and short description to the video using your cell phone number since that's what we want the video to rank for.

Title idea – 555-888-7799 is Nick Carpenter at the Legion of Loan Officers

In the description, you're going to want to put a very similar text making sure that the phone numbers first. I also recommend in the description, putting your phone number in parentheses with no dashes. In case people search it with no dashes, it will show up that way as well.

Description idea – Did you just Google 555-888-7799 or 5558887799? That's me, Nick Carpenter a mortgage advisor with XYZ Company. Call me back!

Leave the video on private when you first upload it and we'll go to the computer to finish the rest.

Go into YouTube and you're going to go to your video library and change it from private to public. But, during that process you're going to add some tags on the video.

Tags are kind of like hashtags or keywords. The two you want to add are your cell phone number with dashes and your cell phone number without dashes.

That's the only two keywords we're adding and you can change it from private to public.

Now, the video is going to be available to be found.

Sometimes it might rank in only a few minutes; sometimes it might rank in a couple of hours. Other times it might take an entire day before that video ranks, but almost every time it will rank in the top three results on Google, which are the most important.

This is a really great way to reinforce who you are and that you're a real person.

Again, they're going to get to see you on video, all your mannerisms and your hand motions and your facial expressions and 100% of your communication in that video.

And when you call them, your voice is already going to be familiar because they will have heard you on video. So now there's a more familiarity in the phone call because of the fact that they've already heard your voice, you're not a stranger voice to them anymore.

So that's what you need to do in order to have a chance to capture more Ghost Clients by making a quick 60 second video for YouTube that ranks for your cell phone number and let's people know exactly who you are.

STRATEGY #16
TEACH CLASSES TO REALTORS

When most loan officers hear the concept that they should be teaching classes to Realtors, the first thing that comes to mind is to talk about their mortgage products. The only idea most loan officers have to teach a room full of real estate agents is updates or new information about loans specific products.

Loan officers want to share the new VA loan limits and changes with the VA loans or they want to share this new down payment assistance program. What happens when you run a class and the goal of the class is to teach mortgage products? It only attracts brand new agents.

The people that come to a class like that, they're not going to typically be great producers and are looking for another way that they can get more loans closed and get more home buyers into homes.

Most of the Realtors who are great agents and who are helping lots of home buyers, they don't have time to come to a class to get better at mortgages. Not only they do not have time to come to a class like that, they don't want to come to a class that teaches them about mortgage products because that's what they rely on a loan officer for.

When you're a mortgage expert, be THE mortgage expert.

You don't need to teach Realtors everything about home loans. Just like Realtors don't teach classes to loan officers about the contract updates and this kind of thing because at the end of the day, it doesn't matter that much to you.

All a Realtor wants to know on the loans is that you have different options, your rates are comparable or competitive and you're going to do what you say. Closing on time is what matters to Realtors. It doesn't matter to them what loan product the client chooses to use as long as you get them the docs to the closing table on time.

When you teach Realtors about mortgage loans and what products are available to the client, they can never say it back the exact same way you do. You're going to give them information that later they will not be able to recite in the same way that you could and it could actually hurt you.

What if they tell a client the information incorrectly about a down payment assistance program or the kind of scores they need or the timeframes-- these kinds of things. Then when you get the client, now you have to start from a negative because you have to correct those things from the beginning.

So, it can actually hurt you to teach Realtors about mortgage products.

A much better idea is to teach Realtors about marketing.

Get a room full of agents and teach them something they can immediately implement or go home and do on their own and see results from that.

Help them get more leads. Help them get more clients. Help them get back in contact with their database.

There are so many ways you can help an agent with their marketing, and by doing that, you're going to demonstrate way more value than any other loan officer.

Realtors always want to grow their business.

At the end of the day, they're in real estate to make money.

If we can show them how to make more money, it's only natural that they're going to come back and say, "okay, what else do you have?"

If you can show them a little trick on how they could capture a few more leads online or convert a couple more clients, or get a couple more referrals...

You're talking about big dollars in real estate.

With an average home in America in 2018 being $255,000, that's makes a 3% commission check about $7650 each. It doesn't take very many ideas or very many new clients and closings to have a significant impact on a Realtor's income.

Imagine for a moment, you could teach a class and share an idea with Realtors to add one deal per month or even one deal every other month to their business.

$255,000 sales price x 3% commission = $7650 x 12 months = $91,800 in additional income over a year.

We're talking about serious money!

Next time you get an opportunity to get in front of a room full of agents, teach them some marketing, share some ideas with them that they can use right away to go and add another deal to their pipeline.

Maybe there's a chance you don't feel like you have enough knowledge or skills to teach Realtor's marketing. In that case, you could bring in a guest. There's nothing wrong with having a guest come in and you host the event and the guest shares information. It's still going to add value to you as a loan officer, but obviously not at the exact same level as if you get in front and you are the instructor and you are the speaker.

Imagine for a moment having 20 or 30 Realtors in a room that's completely packed out. Every seat is full. There are even a couple of people leaning against a wall in the back. I'm pretty sure people call this standing room only.

You have an opportunity to share information and have them listen to you speak for 30 minutes to an hour.

If you share ideas that are fast and easy and get quick results, you're going to have people coming up to you after the class and watch to know how they can partner with you.

An average of 15% of the room will be interested in working with you. So you should be able to convert 2-3 partners from a room of 15-20 Realtors.

What are some different ideas that you could share in a marketing class?

Here are a few examples:

- Share how to get YouTube videos ranked

- How to do keyword research and find out what people are actually searching for on Google and YouTube
- Show them how to have a database marketing plan using Facebook retargeting and email
- Share how they could sell listings faster using social media and modern marketing
- You could teach a class about how to take their database and market only their database using Facebook ads
- Teach a class and show them how to re-target all the people that visit their website
- You could teach a class and show them how to launch their first Facebook ad for a property they have listed
- Teach a class about automation and lead conversion
- You can host a class about scripting and what to say on the phone and what to say in emails and text messages and how often to reach out and what that process looks like
- You could host a class around video marketing and different ways to use video on Facebook
- You can have a class specifically around live videos and doing live videos on Facebook or live videos on

> Instagram and talk about the benefit of doing live videos compared to recording videos

These are some ideas on topics you can teach Realtors.

And again, if you feel like you aren't capable of teaching classes, then you could always bring in a guest speaker.

So, consider adding live events and hosting classes to your marketing plan if it's not already in place.

STRATEGY #17
MONTHLY MARKET UPDATE VIDEO

Every loan officer has a database, but the vast majority are not keeping up a relationship with those people.

The mortgage business has a lot of moving pieces and sometimes it's hard to focus on the people that have already done business with you. So, we rely on our company's drip campaign that is sending out once a week or once a month emails on your behalf.

The challenge is email is not as popular as it once was and people may only be going into their email once a week, once a month, maybe they never really go into their emails and see what's in there, and so your message could be falling on deaf ears.

One of the ways you can increase the results from your weekly database emails is by also mirroring those messages as a Facebook ad.

We all have a database that exists somewhere. It might be inside of the CRM or it might be on an Excel spreadsheet or it could even be inside of Microsoft Outlook. Regardless where your database is, there's a way to export that database to a CSV or TXT file.

Then, we can turn that export into a Facebook custom audience. Now you can run ads to that specific audience you've uploaded. Only the people from your list will see the ad you are paying for on Facebook.

It's a great idea to upload a market update video and run that to your database. How long should it run for? It could be as short as one weekend or as long as the whole month.

The video will be about 1-2 minutes long if you're doing it by yourself or it will be up to 3 minutes if you're doing it with a Realtor partner.

Shorter videos are a little better because you can get more people to watch them all the way to the end.

If you do have a Realtor on the video, I recommend starting with them because people are always more interested in what's going on with houses than they are with what's going on with mortgage loans.

Lead with a Realtor and they can share three pieces of information like...

- What neighborhoods are selling the fastest
- What zip code is the most desirable
- What's the average price per square foot
- Average days on the market
- Average sales price
- Any new trends or things changing in the market
- If it's a buyer or seller's market

Those are some of the kinds of ideas the Realtor can share in the monthly market update video.

Then you as the loan officer can also share some updates about the mortgage side –

- Whether rates are increasing or decreasing
- Where the rates today are compared to historical data

- If there's any new down payment assistance programs or refinances programs
- You can reinforce the message that you serve veterans and there's an opportunity for veterans

These are the kinds of things that you could share on the loan side during the monthly market update video.

Should there be a call to action?

I think the only call to action should be for them to either message you or reach out by a phone call and if they want to chat more about their specific situation or if they have a referral.

I don't think the video on Facebook should have a button and a headline and a link to some place like we do when we run normal ads.

I think it should just be a video going out to your database.

That way it looks like their friend sharing a video on Facebook and not like an advertisement on Facebook.

The monthly market update video can be one of your strategies for retargeting your database.

This is a way you can stay in front of them on Facebook, which we already know people are spending up to 45 minutes per day on Facebook.

So, it makes sense to do your database marketing right where they are already hanging out.

STRATEGY #18
FIVERR VIDEOS AND STUFF

One of the resources I use a lot to get little projects done or fun ideas brought to life is a website that has sellers starting at only $5 each.

This is a great website where you can get things made like videos, hand written art, you can get voiceovers, video transcription, video editing and subtitles. You can also get different graphics made, logos, music, and all kinds of fun things.

Once you go to this website and check it out, sometimes your mind can even run wild with different ideas and how you could use some of those services.

The website I'm talking about is **Fiverr.com** and this is a great resource for you to create fun ways to get Realtors attention.

So for example, when it's a Realtor's birthday, you can have a completely custom birthday rap song and video created for a Realtor for like $20 or $30.

You could also go on there and have custom logos and graphics made or video intros and outros. You can even hire SEO experts.

You can have articles written, you can have your videos transcribed, and there's so many ways that you can use Fiverr when you are starting out your mortgage business or when you don't want to pay an American price in order to get something done. You can take advantage of the economies in different countries and where somebody is really happy to do a project for $5 or $10 that maybe to get somebody in your local area it might cost $50 or $100 to do.

So, it's a way that you can get a lot of things done in a really cheap way.

And, you can also have creative (and sometimes silly) marketing that no one else has.

One of the greatest things you could do for your Realtor partners would be to have some video intros and outros created for them. The intro can have their logo spinning around in the beginning. And then on the outro part, it has their logo plus on their contact information.

Now the Realtor can slap those clips on their videos and make them look a lot more professional.

There are also video editors, so you can actually shoot video, put it in a Google Drive and they will do all the editing for you.

It's services like this where Fiverr is a great resource for you to just stand out with marketing that's really unique and fun and inexpensive to test ideas or trying new things or get some silly project out into the marketplace because it's only going to cost you a few dollars to do it.

Things like marketing flyers, logos and video editing can all be done for just a few dollars a piece on Fiverr.com.

STRATEGY #19
CHAMPAGNE CLOSING

Closing a real estate house is usually a pretty boring process. It's a ton of papers they have to be signed. That leads to a hand cramp and overall it's just not that much of a pleasant experience, but it is a big moment that you can turn into a celebration if you do it correctly.

The champagne closing is one way that you can make the closing table really fun and memorable.

There are a few steps to execute this strategy correctly.

First, you're going to need a small cooler. The size for a 6 or 8 pack is great.

Next, you go to the liquor store and you're going to buy champagne splits. If you're not familiar with that term, it means a small bottle of champagne. It's probably about a third of a normal bottle. Usually it's going to cost around $7 to $15 for the split depending on what brand you buy.

Then, you need to go to Party City or whatever is in your local area for a party supply store and you want to get some plastic champagne glasses. You can usually get the pack that has about 20 glasses in there or 25 glasses for less than $10. You can keep those at your office.

Now in your cooler, when it's time for closing, you're going to want to put the cool champagne with 4 glasses in the

83

cooler and you're going to bring that with you to the closing table.

We'll start getting the supplies out of the cooler when they're finishing with all the papers.

Let's set up the glasses and get the bottle ready. If it has a topper or wrapper, you can take it off.

Then when you're ready, you can put a towel on top and open the bottle.

Now, pour half glasses for the new homeowners, their Realtor and yourself. Now make a toast!

Get somebody to take a photo while you're doing the toast so you have a great photo for Facebook.

You can tag the clients and Realtor in the photo and tell them congratulations. These posts are great to demonstrate success that you're working with people and you're having closings. It will also let all the clients' friends know when they see the tag that they just had a closing and you're their loan officer.

If you use the word CONGRATS, it will push the post out to a few more people as well because Facebook puts a lot of weight into that word.

This is a really cool way by spending about $10 - $15 you can create a very memorable experience by using a split of champagne and a few plastic glasses from a party store.

Plus, you'll have the best type of marketing – Social Proof.

STRATEGY #20
LOTTO TICKET ICEBREAKER

How many hand written note cards do write per week?

Now, I'm not the best at keeping up with it on a weekly or daily basis, but I do totally understand the power and impact that a handwritten note can have.

When was the last time you received a handwritten note?

Just that answer alone will probably tell you how impactful the next one that you receive or the next one that you send out will be to that person.

If you're hosting classes like we talked about in Strategy #16, then the lottery ticket icebreaker is a great follow up strategy after the class is over.

Obviously this is only going to work in states that have scratch off lottery tickets. If your state doesn't have that, think about something else that you might be able to put inside of your note card that would be fun.

You can go to the store grab 10, 20, 50 scratch offs at a time and just have those available in your desk. When you're sending out a handwritten note card, if you want to set yourself up for a phone call afterwards, you can include a lottery ticket.

When you add a lottery ticket you could also play off of the idea on the lottery being 'lucky'. In your text you could say,

"PS, so lucky to meet you" or "I'm so lucky to call you a friend" or "I'm so lucky to have you on my team". Any of these kinds of phrases can be a play off of the lottery ticket.

The whole point of the lottery ticket really is that it makes your note card a little bit more entertaining when they get it in the mail. Right away, there's something fun to do.

It's a chance they could actually win something. I mean, that'd be awesome if they actually won $1,000 or some crazy amount of money off of your scratch off lottery ticket!

But odds are they're not going to win in anything. And in fact, we're kind of banking on that.

Here's what I mean -

The whole point of the lottery ticket is to make a follow-up phone call even easier.

The idea of the lottery ticket is so when you call the person, instead of having this awkward thing where it's obvious that you want to meet with them, you can just start the conversation by laughing with each other.

One of the ways to create a connection on a phone call is laughing together. Laughter is the ultimate sign of people's guard being down. Always take the opportunity to laugh with somebody if you can create that moment. The lottery ticket is how you can engineer this moment.

When you mail the lottery ticket and then you follow-up with a phone call, you can start the conversation like this, "Hey, did you win a million bucks on that lottery ticket or what?"

The person is usually going to come back and tell you, "oh it was a loser" or "I won a dollar".

You can say, "Oh, so I guess that means you're still going to be a Realtor then, huh?"

They'll usually laugh and agree with you.

You'll say, "Awesome. You know what? That's actually why I'm calling you. Thank you again for coming to my class. I've got this marketing checklist where I can figure out different ways I can help you and I wanted to see if we can get together and go over it?"

So the lottery ticket is a really great way, for only $1, to throw in a super fun item into your handwritten note cards.

Now you can have an easy to initiate a conversation by asking the simple question, "Hey, did you win a million bucks on that lottery ticket or what?"

STRATEGY #21
GET A CREDIT REPAIR PARTNER

Many loan officers try to do credit repair themselves or try to find ways to shortcut the process and do a rapid rescore when a client has some credit challenges. The problem is not that you can't do credit repair, but how much time and energy and effort and attention it takes in order for you to do that credit repair.

The other thing is if you either try to do it yourself and you're not as good at it as an actual professional or you don't have a plan in place for credit repair, you're leaving a lot of money on the table.

If you're doing any kind of internet lead generation, then you already know that getting people that have credit challenges is just a normal part of that.

I would say today, we'd probably get at least 20% of the leads that you can generate through Facebook ads or Instagram ads are going to have some sort of credit challenge.

They need some help.

They're going to need a plan and maybe a couple of months in order to just get everything fixed up so that they can get the best rate.

Sometimes people will come to you and they can qualify today but you know they'd be way better off getting their score up a little to get the best programs.

One of the reasons you should have a credit repair partner is so that you always have a plan for any home buyer that comes to you.

Instead of turning away a buyer or you can tell them, this is great, we have a perfect plan for you.

When a buyer comes that has a credit challenge, although we know they can't buy a home right now, eventually they can buy a home.

If they listen to your instructions, we contact your credit partner and they go through the steps necessary there, then they eventually we'll be able to qualify them.

If you know these people will buy a house in three months or six months from now, then why not have a plan for them?

Get excited for the clients and refer them to your credit partner to handle it.

Eventually that business is going to trickle back in and it will be like found money.

In the mortgage business, we're talking about multiple thousand dollars checks that are trickling back in. If you're a broker, maybe those are up to $10,000 in checks, right?

We're talking about real money.

This is one of the reasons why you want to partner with a great, reputable credit repair company in order to make sure that you're getting the business back and those clients are lost in a black hole like most credit companies.

I recommend finding a company that has some ability for you to know what's going on with the clients all the time. Look for a company with a referral partner dashboard to login 24 hours and see what's going on with the clients.

Also, look for one with co-marketing materials that you can use to brand yourself and brand the credit repair company.

Maybe they even have staff making videos you can use to market yourself because sometimes the toughest thing is coming up with the content.

Finally, look for a company who makes it simple to refer them. I prefer one that has a custom link I can use and they know when my clients book an appointment straight from my link.

These are some of the characteristics you might want to look for in a credit repair company.

Today 25-50% of the clients we refer to our credit partner end up signing up and come back to us in 1-6 months ready to buy a house.

Here's another source of exclusive pre-approved home buyers that can be referred to your best Realtor partners.

STRATEGY #22
BECOME THE LOCAL AMBASSADOR

Loan officers and real estate agents are always calling themselves the 'local expert'. One of the ways you can demonstrate being a local expert instead of only saying it, is by becoming and positioning yourself as a local ambassador.

If you think about what does that mean, what would a local ambassador do?

What would their roles and responsibilities be?

It would be to constantly promote that area, right?

If your house and office are in the same neighborhood and you go out to dinner in the same neighborhood, you probably already have enough of a network to begin this positioning.

One simple strategy you can use to become the local ambassador is to have a once a week or once a month Facebook video show.

You can do this by recording the show with a high production value or you could pull your phone out and go live on Facebook with your guest.

If you choose to have a Facebook Live show try to pick the same day and time every week. You can create the same consistency TV sitcoms have where the audience comes to expect it.

If you're releasing high production content, you're probably going to want to shoot these maybe even a couple of weeks in advance. You can hire a videographer for a day and go out and shoot 6, 8, or even 10 of these videos in one day.

Next the videos can be edited down and released out once per week or however you intend to do it.

Facebook Live is great for a more off the cuff kind of person. Pick a day and time and make sure that you're consistent with the live video. That's why I think this only has to be once a week or once a month. Once a week is probably better because it's going to give you an opportunity to spotlight more businesses.

You can also take videos like these and be able to run them as evergreen Facebook ad content. It makes amazing retargeting videos and content to demonstrate your expertise and what's going on inside of your local area to buyers both in your area and to people who are considering moving to the area.

You can post these videos on your branded Facebook page or your community branded page.

What's great about posting the videos on Facebook and then running them as ads is that you can build an audience off of everyone who watches the video.

Now as a loan officer, you have a lot of extra value where you can promote things going on to this built in audience.

People will lift you up as an Ambassador once you claim the position.

When you decide you're going to be the local ambassador, you can go to local businesses and you can shoot some videos and help give them more exposure.

Again, these videos can be done live on Facebook or recorded with a high production value.

The video is a general chat about wh the business owner you're interviewing loves the area, why they decided to have their business here, what's next for them, etc. The owner can even give out a little coupon or some kind of discount for anybody that watches that video for the next week or month.

Then after you have the video on Facebook, you can ask the business owner to share it. That's how you can start getting some exposure into their network by having them share your content.

They can also share the video if they have an email database or anything like that. Your interview is going to make them look and feel great. It's going to make them look good because it's a nice exposure piece, but it's also going to bring some value back to you as the host or the presenter on that video and people might want to find out more information about what you have going on.

You can always have call calls to actions in the video or in the text in terms of if people want to learn more about the business owner or if people want to learn more about working with you to get a home loan.

These are great videos.

Your real estate agents will also love the videos because they know they should be creating content that's locally based and creates value, but they don't know how.

If you take the initiative and you go out into your local area and you create valuable content and you bring that valuable content back out into the market, the Realtors can share your content. They can just share your content. They don't need to go and create their own stuff. Its way simpler for somebody to hit the share button and post the video that you've already made, then they go out and try to recreate and make their own video.

So that's one idea for Loan Officers to use this local ambassador strategy.

You can also be able to have a lot of video content and value for your Realtors to put out on their pages, on their profiles and out to their email databases.

Finally, this all creates a spider web back to you as the original poster of the video and as the host of the video.

So that's why you should consider taking this local ambassador strategy using it in your area.

STRATEGY #23

CONNECTING YOUR PARTNERS TOGETHER / NETWORKING STACK

This is a strategy that I learned from Michael J Maher in his book ***7 Levels of Communication***.

This is my take on a strategy that he shares inside of that book and he calls it Networking Stack Days.

The idea of it is that we're often meeting with Realtors, vendors, friends and referral partners, and business associates in many different disconnect meetings throughout the month.

One way you can connect all your meetings together are in an idea called the networking stack.

Home Base

First, pick a 'Home Base'. This is a restaurant you're always going to use for all your meetings.

You want to get to know the staff and manager well so they get familiar with what you are doing. It's a good idea to do a trial run and help the staff understand your goals and wishes for the day.

They can learn not to come over every 5 minutes and to keep the next guest at the front of the restaurant until exactly the top of the hour.

Imagine having a home base restaurant that you use for meetings where you have the same booth on the same day of the week with the same server and the same manager every time.

These meetings are not about eating a whole meal every time but you could certainly eat breakfast and lunch during the 4-5 hours you're there. It's really about having 45 minutes or one hour together.

As people who are arriving or leaving for these meetings, they're going to be a slight overlap where you have an opportunity to introduce your partners together.

So, if you have five meetings in one day, for example, you have five meetings that start from 10:00 AM and then that would end at 3:00 PM.

I like stacking these meetings so two Realtors never meet each other. It could look like this –

Meeting 1 @ 10am –   Realtor

Meeting 2 @ 11am –   Insurance Agent

Meeting 3 @ 12pm –   Realtor

Meeting 4 @ 1pm –   Divorce Attorney

Meeting 5 @ 2pm –   Realtor

You're able to introduce Realtors to other vendors they may need, but you're not introducing them to other agents. They'll only know the people that they're getting to meet on the two opposite ends. And for every Realtor, that's not going to be another Realtor. It eliminates any perception of you meeting with every agent and that they are not special.

You want them to feel like they're the only agent you're meeting with and everybody else does other things.

Doing the networking stack day is going to allow you to maximize your time because you never leave. There is no commuting time. There's no getting lost using GPS trying to figure out where you'd have to go because everybody is going to come to you.

You're going to get to introduce people together as they are coming and going and that's one way that you can increase your perceived value because high value people create connections. One way that you can become high value is to be able to create more connections.

That's also a great piece of the networking stack because at minimum you'll be creating one new connection with each person. It doesn't have to lead to business for the value to be felt from the connection. The value is the connection, not whether business happens or not.

STRATEGY #24
HOST A FACEBOOK GROUP

Having your own Facebook group is a way you can create your own fishing pond. It's an environment you can control and affect the way people perceive you.

You can have different types of Facebook groups depending on what your end goal is.

As a loan officer, you might have a Facebook group that's designed for **people who live in your local city** or in your specific neighborhood.

Live.Love.Charlotte.

I Love Charlotte Community

The Charlotte West End

Charlotte Locals

These are all examples of what you can call a locally focused group on Facebook.

This type of group can be about what's going on in the area and you can be the only loan officer inside. You can also control which Realtors are inside.

The next type of Facebook you can consider running is one for **home buyers and investors**.

Charlotte Real Estate Network

Charlotte Home Buyers & Investors

Charlotte West End Homes & Deals

Charlotte Real Estate Connection

These are potential names for a real estate focused Facebook group.

This type of group will create a pool of home buyers, potential home sellers and investors that are able to be picked off by your Realtors and then referred to you for a mortgage.

Of course, you are the only Loan Officer inside providing mortgage updates and advice. So it's a way that you can be perceived as one of, if not THE top local market expert, by being the only person inside of the group.

The next kind of Facebook group you could run would be a **group for real estate agents**.

Charlotte Realtor Referral Network

Charlotte Realtor Syndicate

Charlotte Real Estate Expert Mastermind (CREEM)

The Charlotte Real Estate Alliance

Those are some example names for a Realtor focused Facebook group.

Inside you can provide real estate marketing ideas, peer coaching calls, member spotlights and these kinds of value adds. The end goal is to have a pond to fish for new real estate partners for your mortgage business.

It's kind of like having a live class, but you're going to be doing it online inside of a Facebook group.

You can go live in the group. You can share different ideas. You can encourage conversation and ask questions and create polls and these kinds of things inside of your free Facebook group to create value.

Then, maybe once or twice a week, talk about your success with Realtors who work with you are having. There are tons of things you can brag about like lead generation, lead conversion, database marketing, video marketing, and how much more money they are making. We can find ways to brag about your real estate partners and tie their success back to your success.

Realtors who are interested in what you have going on can reach out and attend your classes or partner up on ads or buy a training you have.

But at the end of the day, that is the point is to have a free Facebook group where you're providing value and then somehow turning that into revenue.

The last kind of group would be for **recruiting loan officers and loan partners**.

This strategy is great for mortgage company owners, regional managers or anyone looking to expand their team.

You can open a Facebook group for loan officers where you can do a very similar strategy like we are with the real estate agents. Your group can share different marketing ideas and ways to get Realtor partners. You can host peer coaching so you can have members coach the other members about things they're doing really well. You can also bring in special guests and have different guests come in and do training and teach the group. It's all helping to create value within your free Facebook group.

Your call to action is simple.

"Hey, if you want to learn more about how we're doing all this with our local Realtor partners, just reach out on a private message or book a 15 minute phone call on this link."

You provide value and people who want to know more about that value, they are going to find you.

This is a way to use a Facebook group in order to build your mortgage business by having a mastermind of local loan officers with some different guests or different vendors that are affiliated with the industry.

This group can demonstrate that you're smarter than other loan officers in marketing and you have ways to help them grow their business. Maybe they have lacked the resources or the ideas. You already have it figured out so they can work with you and have that in place in their business.

Having a free Facebook group where you provide value and move people up the ladder of next logical steps will create a new pillar of business for you.

As a loan officer, the main 4 ways you might consider using a free Facebook group would be having a group for local residents, a group for home buyers and investors, a group for Realtors, or a group for loan officer recruiting.

STRATEGY #25

HAVE AN EXPOSURE OFFER LIKE A PODCAST OR A VIDEO SHOW

In Strategy #22, we talked about becoming the Local Ambassador and how you can take your social media platforms, like Facebook and YouTube, and create exposure for local businesses.

This is a very similar strategy, but we're creating an exposure offer specifically for our referral partners and friends. The main two ways you can do this is by having a podcast or weekly video show.

Video Show

If you have a video show, this show can be recorded in a high production value or it could be shot live. You can do the show live on Facebook or you could also do the show live on YouTube and then post it to Facebook or vice versa. Either way, you can download the video and post it to other sites and cross post, that kind of thing.

A video show should not be about you. It's about other people. It's the partner spotlight. It's about your referral partners and it's about great experts.

It's not about your mortgage business. It's not about how you help your referral partners when you name the show.

Of course you can give yourself a plug during the video, but in the actual name, you want it to be bigger than just you.

What's cool is you can go live on Facebook from your cell phone. Turn your phone horizontally and go live on your personal profile or your business page.

The person you're going to have on as a guest will watch your Facebook live from their phone and you will be able to invite them to join you.

Doing it this way is going to put you both side by side as equals in the video screen whereas if you do it on a vertical cell phone, one person is going to be big and the other person is going to be the picture-in-picture small version and it's not going to look nearly as good. That's why you want to make sure you do any Facebook lives with a guest from a horizontal cell phone.

Now when you go live on Facebook, you can ask them some general questions like –

- How did they get started
- Why did they decide to be a Realtor
- Tell us about their first deal
- What would they say to someone else starting now
- What did they learn in their first year
- The craziest deal they have done

Of course this is more on the real estate side of things and you can change these questions up depending on what industry your guest is from.

Remember that you want to try to inject in some humor too.

Find ways to ask about their crazy experience, their funniest experience, weirdest experience, and weirdest clients.

That's the one thing missing from a lot of marketing today is humor. Everybody wants to be super serious. Give your referral partners a chance to kind of show off a little bit, and then in the greatest way, you want to lift them up and give them exposure so other people who enjoy them and their personality can also decide they want to do business together.

Having a video show is a great thing you can offer Realtors and referral partners. You can send the guest a message with the link and they will share it to their network.

They're going to give you some great words of edification whenever they share the video and talk about how great you are. These videos are going to help you and the guest at the same time.

Podcast

The other way you can offer people exposures is by having a podcast.

In 2019, Google is the #1 search engine, YouTube is #2 and iTunes is #3. Having a podcast will give you another horse in the race to be in front of potential clients.

What's really interesting is if you have a podcast and you invite people onto your show, very few people will ask you anything about how many listens you get or how many viewers or subscribers you have.

Very few people will ask you that because it's simply the fact that you've been invited.

That is the greatest honor in itself.

Having a podcast is one way you can give people that honor.

You can start a podcast using several different online platforms. Two of the easiest today are BlogTalkRadio.com and Anchor.fm.

Both of those are really simple.

You can operate them from a phone or from a computer and be able to record podcast content and then post that to your actual podcast.

Both of those platforms can be syndicated to iTunes and Stitcher and other places that people like to listen to podcasts.

Having a podcast or video show that you can invite referral partners or vendors or friends and people you like and want to get exposure for is an amazing way that you can initiate the Law of Reciprocity.

STRATEGY #26
HELP REALTORS WITH LEADS

Almost every loan officer has the same pitch to real estate agents today and that's why everyone appears as equals. It's very difficult to position yourself apart from your competition if you just say the same thing as they say.

For example, many loan officers have a pitch like, I have the best rates, the best term times, I close on time, I have great communication, I get the docs to closing early...and this is what every loan officer's says.

That's why if you say it, there's nothing different about what you're saying compared to every other loan officer in your market.

You need to have some way to actually differentiate yourself, and one of the best ways is to help realtors generate leads.

If you can figure out ways to generate home buyer leads before they go to a Realtor, you can have the power to refer those buyers back to any agent that you choose. When you help a Realtor with leads, you can also help them take back control away from some of these big aggregators.

There companies are totally molesting the real estate industry and taking full advantage of Realtors and you can take the power back to the agent, away from the big aggregators like Zillow.com, Realtor.com and Trulia.com.

You can also help agents get the power back from agencies that are overcharging super inflated prices for home buyer leads. At the end of the day, you can generate the same kind of leads for only a few dollars that they can charge over $100 for.

That's why these sites love to get people locked into contracts. Even if you figure out how to generate your own leads for $1 or $2 each, you're still in a contract for leads costing $65, $80 and even up to $100 per lead.

How can I be so confident these are the same leads?

My friends sell to those aggregators. That's right. When the big sites have slow times they will buy leads from other providers like us.

Today, one of the easiest ways to generate leads is using Facebook and Instagram ads.

Facebook has made the Ads Manager pretty easy to use and they will even give you suggestions of other interests and keywords that you could target based on what you're already telling them.

Some of the targeting options available in the Facebook Ads Manager include –

- Realtor.com
- Trulia
- Zillow
- House hunting
- Buying and selling real estate
- Mortgage brokers
- Getting pre-qualified (for a loan)

All these targets are available inside of Facebook Ads Manager. They make it super simple today to launch ads.

Another thing that's cool is Facebook owns Instagram so when you create ads inside the Facebook Ads Manager, you can also launch ads on Instagram at the same time. You can manage both platforms from the same ad management tool versus having different places to go for each one.

Leads on Facebook are going to convert at different rates depending on what type of ad you're running.

For example, in The Legion of Loan Officers, the first campaign we teach is called the training wheels campaign A.K.A. the Realtor Getter. It's generating thousands of leads across America every month for less than $2 on average. These leads are cheap and they convert around 2.5% from new leads to mortgage pre-approvals.

Our advanced Facebook funnels and long form leads will cost more, around $5 each, but they also convert at a higher rate. You can get 1 pre-approval from every 10 leads in most cases.

Personally I think there is a balance in running high quantity funnels and high quality funnels. It will keep the database growing at a fast rate and also get the most pre-approvals for right now business.

Helping Realtors with Facebook ads or helping Realtors generate leads for their real estate business is one of the best ways that you can provide value to an agent and demonstrate that you're an actual partner in their business and not just sitting back waiting for them to bring the leads to you. It's a powerful in your face strategy to go out and generate leads and business opportunities for Realtors to talk to.

When you generate your own leads, you also have the chance to generate listing appointments for Realtors. And let me tell you, there is nothing more powerful than generating listing appointments for an agent to create loyalty with their loan partner.

No loan officers really care about generating listing appointments. And, I'm not even suggesting that you should care about that either, but just know that if you're generating buyer leads, naturally some of those buyer leads are also going to be seller leads.

I don't know what the percentage is today, but maybe 10-25% or more of the leads we get on Facebook who are buying a house also have to sell a house.

If those numbers hold true in your local market it would mean that for every 10 leads you generate on Facebook, at least one of them is going to have a house to sell.

Generating our own leads up front creates so much control because you can create a golden handcuff scenario so Realtors never want to leave you and lose the easy business.

STRATEGY #27
USE A MARKETING CHECKLIST

Its commonplace for Realtors to meet with you once and then become a ghost. One of the greatest tools you can use to get them to come back is a marketing checklist.

Inside The Legion of Loan Officers, we created a 21 point marketing checklist that our members use to ask yes or no questions to Realtors and figure out where they are strong and where they are weak in marketing. Everybody has strengths and everybody has weaknesses when it comes to marketing. Sometimes we can help to improve where we're weak and exponentially grow where we're strong by having an extra set of eyeballs take a look at what we are doing.

You can create a simple checklist using Microsoft Word or Google Docs with 10 to 30 questions. Each question should be designed to figure out what a Realtor is doing or not doing in terms of marketing.

Some example questions that we ask are –

- Do you have a Facebook business page?
- When is the last time you posted it on the page?
- How often are you running Facebook ads?
- How many video testimonials did you get last month?
- Has your entire database heard your voice in the past 30 days?

- Do you have the FB pixel installed on your website?

Notice these are all simple questions designed to help understand what they're doing and what are some really fast ways that we could impact their business. It's quicker to give a big boost in an area they are weak vs. making a small impact where they are already strong.

If you can take somebody that has nothing in one area and you can jump them up to a level 3 or 4 in that area, that's going to be a bigger impact than making a one number improvement in something that they're already pretty good at.

That to me is the value of the checklist.

You can find out where Realtors are strong and you can find out where Realtors are weak without them having to tell you that they're weak in those areas. They can just answer yes or no.

Then you can use your checklist as a way to get Realtors to come back for another meeting. If you've ever had a Realtor come to a first meeting and then ghost you, you know that that's a very common occurrence today.

Realtors will meet with a loan officer once, maybe grab some coffee or a lunch, and then disappear. Having a checklist is going to keep their realtor engaged and it's going to keep them coming back.

The best way to use the checklist that I have found is to bring it out at the end of your first 1-2-1 meeting with a Realtor. You'll have just enough time to go over the checklist but not enough time to go deep into how you can help them. That's the goal for the next meeting. And, it's why the Realtor won't ghost you because they want to hear what you can do.

Piquing a Realtor's curiosity is an important step most Loan Officers can't include in a one meeting close.

Piquing their curiosity is a lot like what TV shows do to us at the end of each episode. They call them 'open loops' where they open a story before the commercial break or at the end of an episode and now you're like, oh my gosh, what's going to happen on the next one?

The same thing happens to Realtors when we complete the checklist at the end of a meeting. You create an open loop for the agent. Now they want to come back and meet with you again on the checklist in order to close that loop.

Consider using a 10-30 question checklist as a way to ask questions and figure out what are some of the easiest, fastest ways you can provide marketing value to a Realtor to demonstrate you have knowledge and you're a real partner that is going to help them grow their business.

STRATEGY #28
OPEN HOUSE SURVIVAL KIT

I met the home inspector I still refer today because he brought me an 'open house survival kit' when I was working a Sunday afternoon open house back when I was a Realtor in 2007. This was in Mansfield, Texas, and the guy's name is Jeff Mutchler. He's still a home inspector in the Dallas-Fort Worth market with Northstar Home Inspection (northstarhi.com).

Jeff came into the open house I was at and he brought me a bag full of things. I want to share with you some of the ideas he had in his bag and how this could be a way for you to make an impression with a Realtor.

Never show up at a Realtor's open house with empty hands or only a business card.

Here is what Jeff included in his Open House Survival Kit –

- Little notepad
- 2 branded pens
- One can of coke
- One bottle of water
- Some chocolate candy
- A kind bar or multigrain bar
- A company brochure
- 3 business cards

While I don't think this is the #1 strategy to put in place, it is very effective if your business is slow and you want some face time with agents.

Bringing an Open House Survival Kit is a much better way to show up since we know Loan Officers are going to open houses. Now, you're showing up with gifts. You can implement the law of reciprocity by coming in with gifts and giving them things first.

In this case, the biggest thing that the Realtor can offer you back probably is their attention and a little bit of their time.

You do want to make sure if you're going into an open house that you're not being a distraction or a bother. If they have visitors coming into the open house, you want to make sure you sit back or support the Realtor at the open house and not be obtrusive or obnoxious while they're trying to do their job and get some home buyers on the hook.

The Open House Survival Kit can also be a way that you introduce Strategy #26 and the fact you help your Realtors generate leads.

"Hey, how was the traffic been at the open house today? Did you run a Facebook ad for the open house? Is that something that you'd like my help with next week?"

Using the Open House Survival Kit lets you come in with gifts, come in with ideas, strategies, and suggestions.

Help the Realtor understand you are a real partner. You are not a taker. You're out there actively working on getting leads yourself too.

STRATEGY #29
OFFICE SITE VISIT SETUP

I always like to give credit where it's due and this is a strategy I learned while running the marketing department for Benchmark Mortgage down in Plano, Texas. At the time, Benchmark was doing about $2 billion worth of loans per year and we would actively recruit maybe one branch per month or one branch every other month. They were very selective with how they did their recruiting to keep the company culture correct.

One of the pieces to recruiting a Branch Manager was called a Site Visit. This was the first time the person had been to the corporate office and we had a 1 day experience they would go through to understand why they should join us.

The Site Visit is something you could take and implement in your branch and in your personal office as well.

What's the goal?

It's to create conversations you want to create.

You can also make somebody feel like a VIP right from the very beginning and for the whole time they're with you.

Here are a few strategies that you can use during a site visit to make it ultra effective -

VIP Status

First, you want to make the Realtor feel like a VIP from the very beginning. You can do this a couple of different ways. One idea is to have a reserved parking space with their name on it. If it's possible for you to have reserved parking spaces, you could have a sign made that has a slot that you could slide a name plate into the slot whenever people are coming to your office. Print out a paper with their name on it and you could slide it into the sign so that now they have their own reserved parking space.

Another thing you can do is have a sign on your receptionist's welcome desk so they have a welcome sign when they walk into the building.

Or, if you have a TV in your lobby or reception area, you could also have something on the TV welcoming the Realtor to your office.

2. Celebrity Recognition

The second thing you can do to make Realtors feel ultra special when they are coming through your office is have people on your staff already know who they are.

If you think about the President of the United States, if he was going to come to your office and he was going to be taking a tour of your office, everybody would already know who he is, right?

You would not have to introduce him.

People would be going up to him and saying, "Hey, Mr. President, so glad to meet you. Loved your speech last week." Right?

That's the kind of reception we want for the Realtors as well.

The way you can engineer this response is by going to their Facebook profile and printing off the last one or two most recent photos of them. You want to show the people in your office the photos with the Realtor's name and what company they are from.

Now everyone will be prepared when you are walking around the office with a Realtor. This is when it needs to be all hands on deck to work as a team. As you're coming up to anyone in the office, they can get up and say, "Hey John, so nice to meet you, Nick's been telling us so much about you, man, I'd love to do business with in the future. Let us know how we can help you."

It's a totally different approach than when you have to go into the room and introduce the Realtor.

We want to give the impression of 'I already know how you are' and that will make the Realtor feel so special.

3. Photo Props

The third thing you want to do for a Site Visit is to have photos hanging up that allow you to create the conversations you want to create.

So if you do charity work, for example, you should have photos hanging in your office of charity events or different things that you guys have done. It gives you a stopping point to talk about those events when you walk a Realtor around the office.

So you can say, "hey, this photo right here is from when we did this charity event in Dallas, Texas and it was awesome. Man, I'll never forget how we helped this family get a new house for free."

You also want to demonstrate success with clients. So next you want to have some client photos. This could be a chance to tell a crazy client story or a really memorable transaction.

Have you helped anybody of influence? You want to have a photo with them also. This includes politicians, musicians, actors, local business owners and more.

If you've helped a city council member, the mayor, a famous business person, a famous person, politician, anybody in your local area where having them on the wall would mean something to a Realtor coming through, then throw a photo up on the wall and create a talking point.

What this says is if this famous person trusts me, I hope that I can earn your trust as well. You're able to take some of the trust people have of that celebrity and transfer some of it over to yourself as well.

The goal with the photos is to show 3 levels - charity work, helping people and knowing people.

STRATEGY #30
BE A TREASURE CHEST OF IDEAS

Can we be honest about expectations going into a Realtor-Lender relationship? Real estate agents aren't expecting you to have marketing knowledge and ideas to share with them.

They're just expecting to have the mortgage taken care of with competitive fees and rates and close on time. Realtors want you to communicate well, fund fast, and attend your closings. These are normal expectations of Realtors when it comes to partnering with lenders.

One of the ways you can go above and beyond this standard list of qualities is to become a treasure chest of ideas. What I mean by that is to have lots of different strategies and ideas that you can use to help your Realtors grow their business.

You don't want to be a one trick pony where the only thing you know how to do is just to close the loan.

There are so many ways to bring value to the table around topics like paid marketing, organic marketing, video strategies, social media, email marketing, database marketing, and those kinds of things.

All these are opportunities for Realtors to grow their business. You can level up in terms of how Realtors perceive you by knowing about these topics. What makes the knowledge even more of a tool is if you have put it into practice. Demonstration is exponentially more powerful than words.

Want to move in on a Realtor that you've always wanted to work with but you know they have a loan partner already?

This is one of the ways is by having more ideas and more value to bring to the table than whoever they're currently working with.

Assuming that all things are equal and you and the Loan Officer they're currently doing business with both have similar rates, close on time, communicate effectively, and all of these things, the Realtor is going to work with the person that they know, like and trust the most and who brings the most value to the relationship.

This process of demonstrating value usually takes some time and will not be a onetime effort or happen overnight. You can slowly start to become a person of value that the Realtor knows and trusts. That's how you slide in and become the #1 referral partner for a Realtor that you don't currently do business with.

Become a treasure chest of ideas.

One of the best ways you can do that is by joining different Facebook groups, mastermind programs and by putting yourself around people who are doing marketing and are trying new things and are willing to share what works.

Becoming a treasure chest of ideas is going to make you even more valuable to your Realtors than whoever they're working with today or than any Loan Officer that could come along in the future and want to steal them away from you.

You can create this sort of 'golden handcuff' where the Realtor knows he or she will lose all your leads and ideas and knowledge if they ever leave you.

STRATEGY #31
SURROUND YOURSELF WITH WINNERS

You become the average of the five people spend the most time with according to the late Jim Rohn. I don't think this only applies to your physical life. It is also true from your online friends.

In 2005 I left the Air Force because I didn't want to go back to Iraq again. I knew the military wasn't my life path. It was a stepping stone. So I got out when my enlistment was up.

Anyone who has been in the military knows there is a deep and immediate sense of belonging and friendship.

In fact, I had searched for that feeling in the civilian world for years.

The bond.

The brotherhood.

The friendship.

The support and camaraderie.

In 2017, I had 12 years of dedicating myself to mastering real estate and mortgage marketing. Plus, I've be lucky to learn under some amazing mentors.

The Legion of Loan Officers (LegionofLoanOfficers.com) was created at the beginning of 2017 as a platform to give smart mortgage professionals the power back in marketing and to attract 10 additional Realtor referral partners sending you the majority of their deals.

Here are a couple cool stories from members in The Legion -

Joanna Grew a $50MM Mortgage Team

A California loan officer joined The Legion of Loan Officers (LOLO) in 2018 and was averaging around $2 million per month in closed loan volume. She has mainly used two of our strategies – The training wheels campaign and the FTHB campaign – and she has been able to average $4.2 million per month now.

Her team is on track to close $50MM per year now.

Her business has increased so much that she left her retail bank and opened a mortgage brokerage under her own brand and now has a 7 figure annual income business.

Solo Broker Closing 3 Times More Loans Now

Nathan joined The Legion at a time when he was considering leaving the mortgage business. He was burned out on chasing Realtors to close $500k or $600k per month in loans. It wasn't enough for the stress and headaches.

After joining LOLO, Nathan is now closing over $2 million per month in home loans consistently. He does not have a big inflated team with just him and a full time loan processor.

Nathan is now running well over a half million dollar annual income business and doing it partners he enjoys.

New Mortgage Broker Grows Big Team in 12 Months

Reed joined The Legion of Loan Officers about a month after opening his mortgage brokerage in a new state his family moved to.

He has gone from starting with zero business to now having a big, thriving company with 4 full time loan officers, a full time processor, and an Inside Sales Agent converting appointments from their average 1,000 home buyer leads per month.

28 Year Old "Kid" Opens His Own Mortgage Company

Caton was only 27 years old when he joined The Legion with a goal to learn Facebook ads and control his own marketing. He quickly grew his origination business and even got a four figure monthly marketing budget from his company.

Caton had more than tripled his business and opened his own national mortgage company along with another Legion member in 2019.

Legion Member Gets The #1 Realtor in His Market

Michael is a lender in Massachusetts and recently shared a story how he was able to partner with the #1 real estate team in his local market.

It just so happens that this agent used to do business with a colleague in Michael's office but he has switched because of the exclusive leads and other value Michael shares since joining LOLO.

These are just 5 examples of what happens to smart mortgage professionals after joining The Legion of Loan Officers.

You can get started at **http://OneAgentAway.com** and take control of your marketing with training and support for:

- Facebook paid ads
- Facebook organic marketing
- Internet lead phone scripts
- Lead conversion automation software
- Short form leads using Facebook forms
- Long form survey leads
- Facebook messenger bots and funnels
- Hosting live events
- Video marketing (live and recorded)
- Attracting inbound Realtor partners
- Authority building and positioning
- Becoming a published author
- TV / News / Media appearances
- Instagram paid ads
- Snapchat paid ads
- YouTube organic domination
- Database marketing and farming
- Retargeting ads
- Omnipresent marketing
- Sales and scripting
- Getting video and written client testimonials
- Podcasting with iTunes
- And more...

The Legion of Loan Officers is a living, breathing organization that evolves with the times and current strategies. As the next changes happen, we will too.

Get started today at

http://OneAgentAway.com

Connect with Nick Carpenter:

Facebook.com/nillanick

Facebook.com/thenickcarpenter

Instagram.com/beardedmarketer

YouTube.com/nillanicktv

Linkedin.com/in/nicholauscarpenter

Made in the USA
Middletown, DE
29 June 2019